Contents

 Fiction

Dare
page 2

 **Non-fiction**

Scared
page 18

Written by
Dee Reid

Illustrated by
Dylan Gibson

Series editor **Dee Reid**

Before reading Dare

Characters

Cam

Ellie

The headteacher

Killer

Tricky words

- scared
- assembly
- front
- scream
- laughing
- students
- everyone
- busy

Read these words to the student. Help them with these words when they appear in the text.

Introduction

Cam and Ellie are friends. Ellie loves to think up cool tricks to play and she persuades Cam to join in. Cam is not so sure about Ellie's tricks. They usually end up with Cam getting into big trouble. One day Ellie took her pet spider, Killer, into assembly. She persuaded Cam to show Killer to the girl sitting in front of them.

"This is Killer, my pet spider," said Ellie. "But don't be scared, he won't bite! We can play a trick with Killer."

"Show Killer to that girl in front," said Ellie. "No way!" said Cam. "She might scream and I might get into big trouble!"

"Go on," said Ellie. "I dare you!"

The boy next to the girl looked to see what was going on.
Then he saw Killer.
He jumped out of his seat and tried to push his way out of the hall.

The girl next to the boy saw Killer and she screamed.

The girl next to her looked to see why she was screaming.
Then she saw Killer and she began to scream too.

Then everyone began jumping up and screaming.

Cam was laughing so he did not see that the headteacher had come over to the screaming students.

"What is going on?" said the headteacher.

But everyone was too busy screaming and trying to get out of the hall. Then one girl said, "That boy has got a big spider."

Quiz

Text comprehension

Literal comprehension
p6 What was Ellie's trick?
p8 Why did the first girl not scream?

Inferential comprehension
p6 Why do you think Cam does as Ellie asks?
p13 Why does the headteacher think Cam is to blame?
p16 Why doesn't Ellie own up?

Personal response
- Why do you think some people are scared of spiders?
- Is there a creature you are afraid of – snakes, big dogs?

Word knowledge

p4 Find four examples of punctuation.
p5 Find a word that rhymes with 'hated'.
p9 Find three action verbs.

Spelling challenge

Read these words:

came   why   what

Now try to spell them!

Ha! Ha! Ha!

What do you call two spiders who have recently got married?

Newlywebs!

Before reading Scared

Find out about

- things that people are scared of, such as spiders or snakes or heights.

Tricky words

- scared
- heights
- building
- mountain
- special
- enemies
- programme
- celebrities

Read these words to the student. Help them with these words when they appear in the text.

Introduction

Most people are scared of something. Some people are scared of animals. Some people are scared of heights. Some people are scared of spiders. If they see a spider in their home they freeze with fear. But people are a lot bigger than spiders, so why are some people scared of them?

scared

Most people are scared of something.
Some people are scared of some animals.
Some people are scared of heights.
Is there something you are scared of?

Spiders

Some people are scared of spiders. If they see a spider in their home they freeze with fear.

But most spiders don't hurt people
and people are a lot bigger than spiders,
so why are some people scared of spiders?

Snakes

Some people are scared of snakes. If they just see a picture of a snake or a snake on TV, they freeze with fear.

But a picture of a snake or a snake on TV can't hurt you.
So why are some people so scared?

Some people are scared of heights.
If they are high up on a building or
a mountain, they don't like to look down.

They feel like they are going to fall.
Even if there is no way they could fall,
they are still scared.

ROOM 101

NINETEEN EIGHTY FOUR
GEORGE ORWELL

In a book called '1984' the hero had to face the thing he was most scared of.
The hero hated rats.
He was made to go into a special room called Room 101.
His enemies sent rats along a tube to eat him.

There was a TV programme called 'Room 101'.
Celebrities had to say what was the thing they hated most.
Then that thing was put into Room 101.

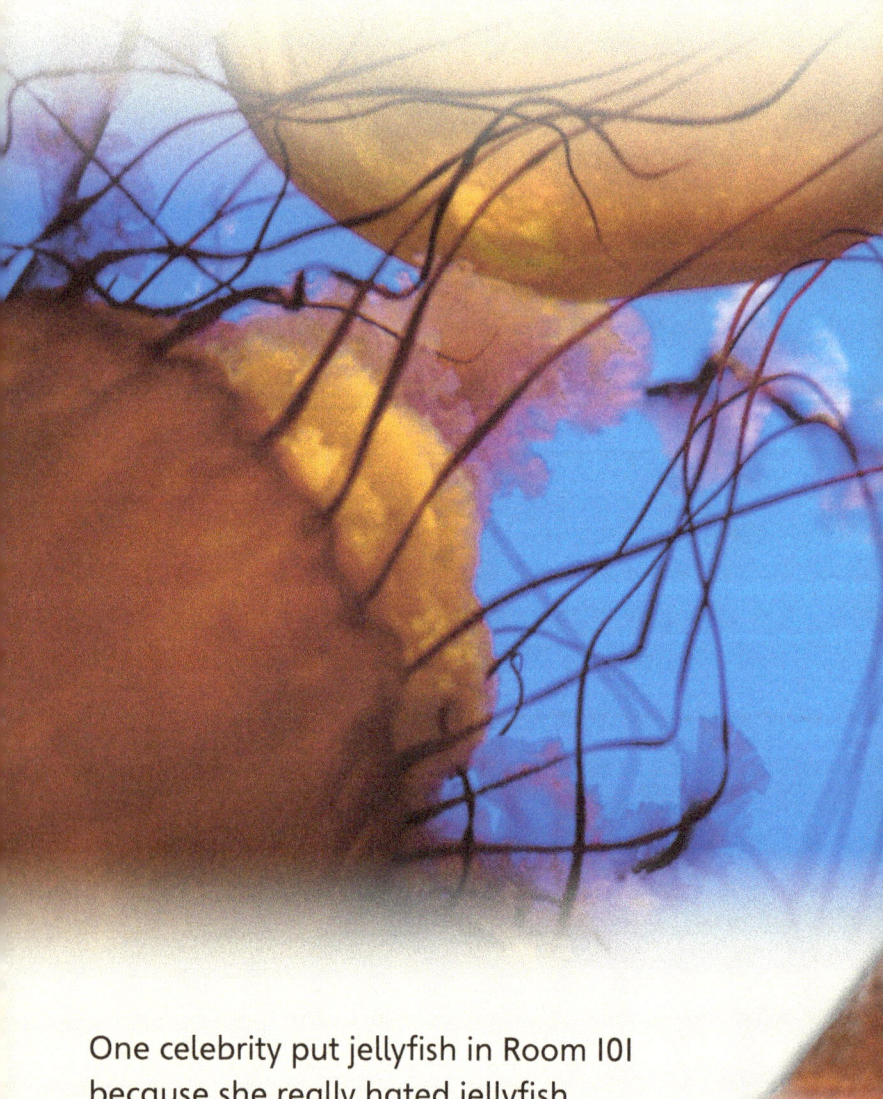

One celebrity put jellyfish in Room 101 because she really hated jellyfish.

One celebrity put slugs in Room 101 because she really hated slugs.

Is there something that you are scared of?
What would you put in Room 101?
Would you put spiders or snakes in Room 101?
Would you put rats or jellyfish or slugs in Room 101?

Some people might say that the thing they hate most is school! Would you put school in Room 101?

Quiz

Text comprehension

Literal comprehension
p20 What do some people do if they see a spider in their home?
p25 Why are some people scared of heights?

Inferential comprehension
p21 Why is it not sensible to be scared of spiders?
p27 What is the purpose of Room 101?
p25 Why is it usually foolish to be scared if you're high up on a building?

Personal response
- How do you think people get over their fear of spiders or snakes?
- Have you sometimes had to pretend you're not scared of something, when really you are scared?

Word knowledge

p20 Find a word that means 'terrified'.
p23 Which two words are contracted in 'can't'?
p30 What do you notice about all these sentences?

Spelling challenge

Read these words:

told   who   across

Now try to spell them!

Ha! Ha! Ha!

What did the spider say to the bee?

Your honey or your life!